This library edition published in 2012 by Walter Foster Publishing, Inc.
Walter Foster Library
Distributed by Black Rabbit Books.
P.O. Box 3263 Mankato, Minnesota 56002

Printed in Mankato, Minnesota, USA by CG Book Printers, a division of Corporate Graphics.

First Library Edition

Library of Congress Cataloging-in-Publication Data

Learn to draw dinosaurs / illustrated by Jeff Shelly.
    pages cm
 ISBN 978-1-936309-48-1
 1. Dinosaurs in art--Juvenile literature. 2.
Drawing--Technique--Juvenile literature. I. Shelly, Jeff, illustrator.
II. Walter Foster (Firm)
 NC780.5.L43 2012
 743.6--dc23
                                                        2011047382

052012
17679

9 8 7 6 5 4 3 2 1

learn to draw

DINOSAURS

Learn to draw and color 27 prehistoric creatures, step by easy step, shape by simple shape!

Illustrated by Jeff Shelly

GETTING STARTED

When you look closely at the drawings in this book, you'll notice that they're made up of basic shapes, such as circles, triangles, and rectangles. To draw all your favorite dinosaurs, just start with simple shapes, as you see here. It's easy and fun!

CIRCLES are used to draw this dino's chest, hips, and "sail."

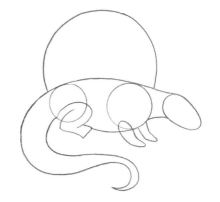
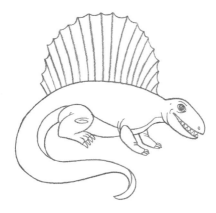

RECTANGLES are good for drawing blocky or boxy heads on dinosaurs.

TRIANGLES are best for drawing dinos with pointed heads.

COLORING TIPS

When you're ready to bring your prehistoric creatures to life on paper, just add a little color with crayons, markers, or colored pencils. Because no one really knows what colors dinosaurs were, get creative with greens, oranges, purples, or any other colors you like!

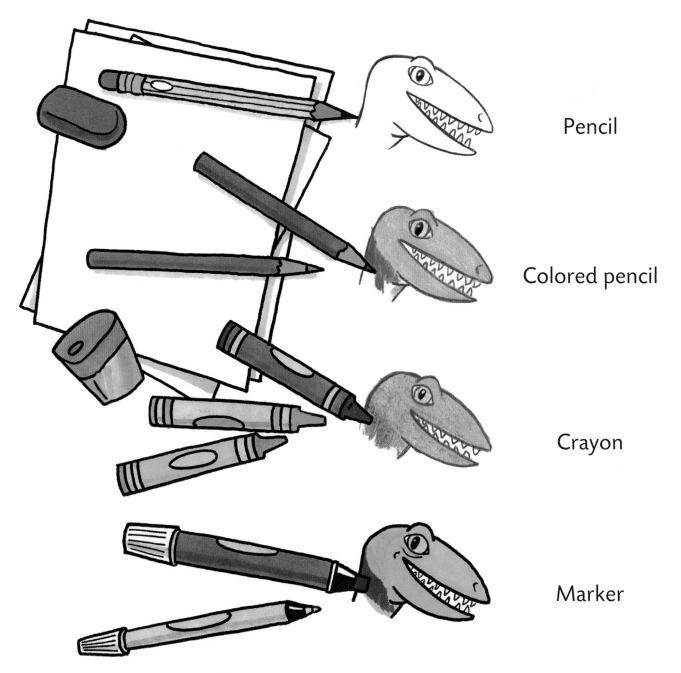

Pencil

Colored pencil

Crayon

Marker

COMPSOGNATHUS

The compsognathus was built for speed!
A pointed head, strong legs, and a long tail
all helped make this dino quick on its feet.

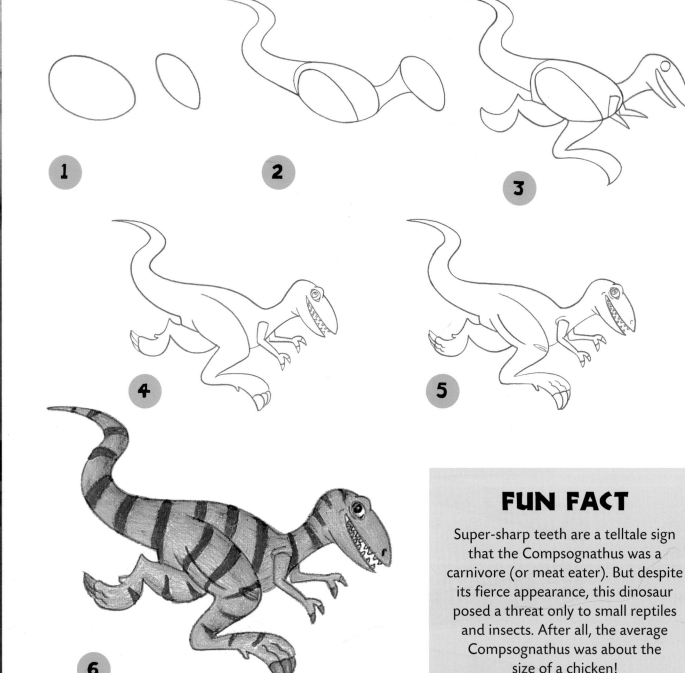

1

2

3

4

5

6

FUN FACT

Super-sharp teeth are a telltale sign that the Compsognathus was a carnivore (or meat eater). But despite its fierce appearance, this dinosaur posed a threat only to small reptiles and insects. After all, the average Compsognathus was about the size of a chicken!

ORNITHOMIMUS

Ornithomimus means "bird mimic," so it should come as no surprise that this dinosaur's neck and legs were shaped like those of an ostrich!

1

2

3

4

MYTH

All dinosaurs lived at the same time.
Fact: In the 165 million years from the dinosaurs' first appearance 230 million years ago to their "disappearance" 65 million years ago, many different species co-existed—but not every species existed during the same time period.

5

6

PROTOCERATOPS

The slow-moving Protoceratops was heavy and round. It relied on a thick helmet and pointed beak to fight off predators.

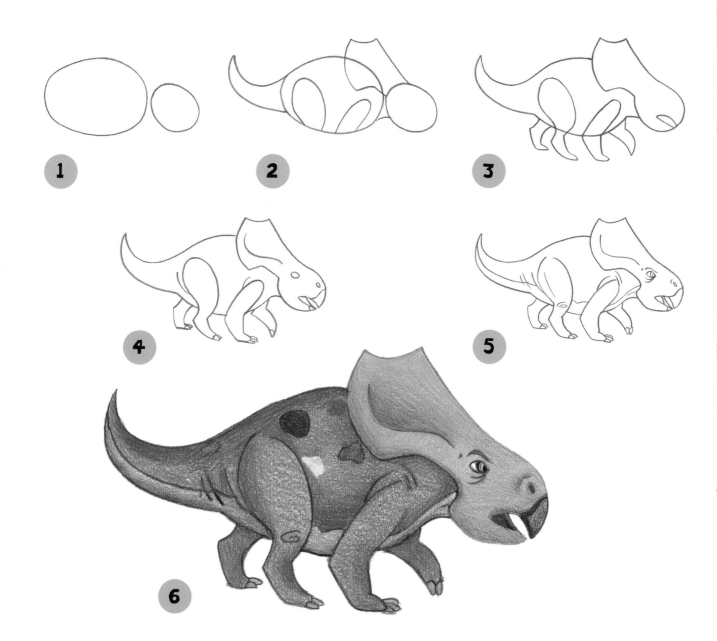

FUN FACT

The first dinosaur eggs ever found by humans belonged to a Protoceratops! Female Protoceratops made small circular holes in the sand. There they laid their eggs, covering them with sand to keep them warm until they hatched.

IGUANODON

The Iguanodon walked on all fours,
but it could stand briefly on its strong back legs
and use its "hands" to gather food.

BRACHIOSAURUS

With tall legs, a long neck, and large nostrils on its head, this plant eater was able to find leaves and fruit that other dinos couldn't reach.

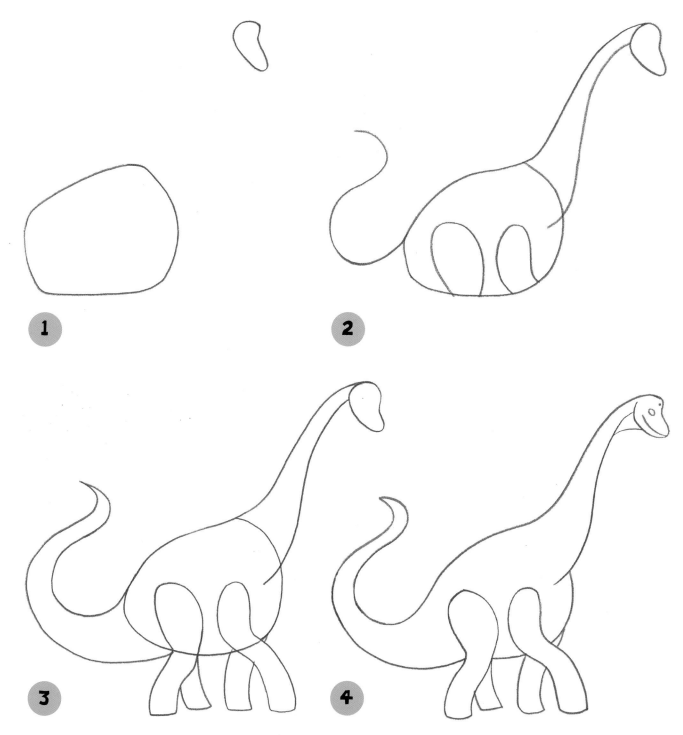

1

2

3

4

5

6

QUETZALCOATLUS

There was more to this flying lizard than wingspan!
The Quetzalcoatlus had a compact,
bean-shaped body, a long neck, and a beak.

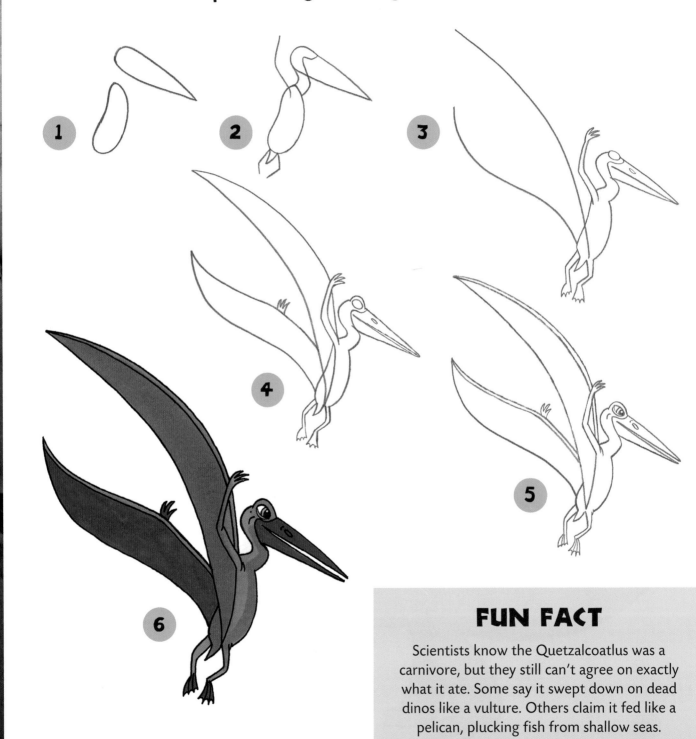

FUN FACT

Scientists know the Quetzalcoatlus was a carnivore, but they still can't agree on exactly what it ate. Some say it swept down on dead dinos like a vulture. Others claim it fed like a pelican, plucking fish from shallow seas.

LAMBEOSAURUS

The Lambeosaurus had a rounded back, a thick tail, and strong hind legs. The purpose of its head ornament remains a mystery.

MYTH

There were 700 types of dinosaurs. Fact: Experts have identified about 700 different dinosaurs, but there may have been many more. After all, in 1842, we knew of only 3 dinosaurs: Megalosaurus, Iguanodon, and Hylaeosaurus!

STYRACOSAURUS

To draw the heavy Styracosaurus, begin with a heart-shaped head and a round body. Later be sure to add its horn and six-spike frill.

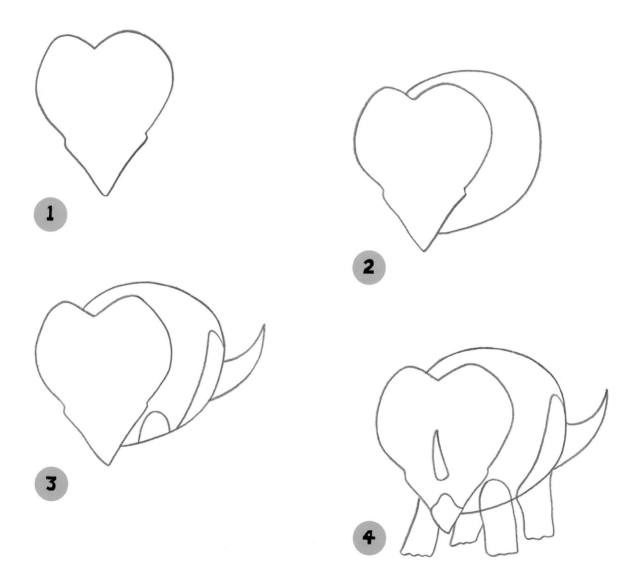

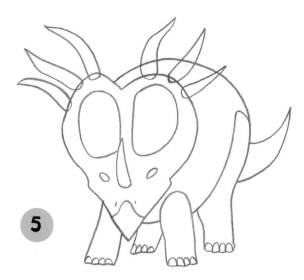

5

6

7

8

TROÖDON

Lightweight and quick, the Troödon was a master carnivore. It was named "wounding tooth" for its mouth full of sharp, jagged teeth!

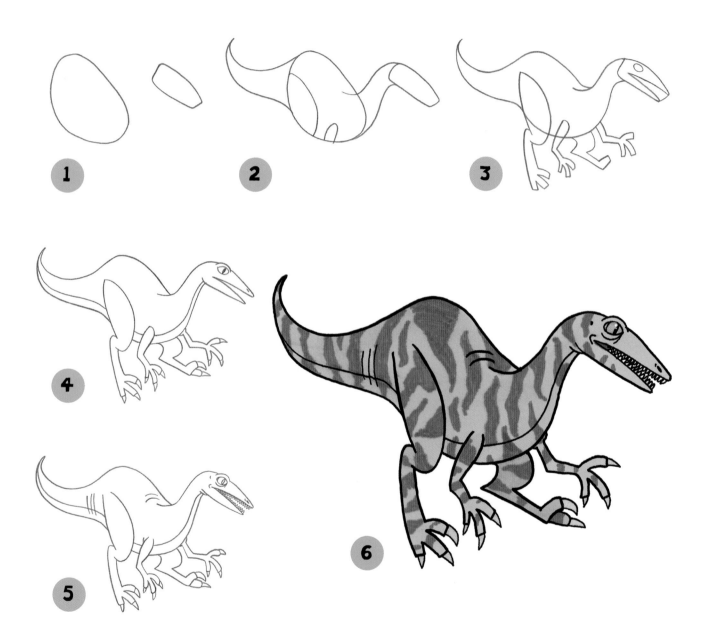

FUN FACT

The Troödon was a biped, meaning that it walked on two feet. Standing tall, this dinosaur's height ranged from 6.5 to 11 feet. But because of its hollow bones, the Troödon probably weighed only about 110 pounds.

ALLOSAURUS

Draw this sauropod-eating carnivore
with a strong neck, sturdy legs, and a powerful tail.
Don't forget the sharp teeth and claws!

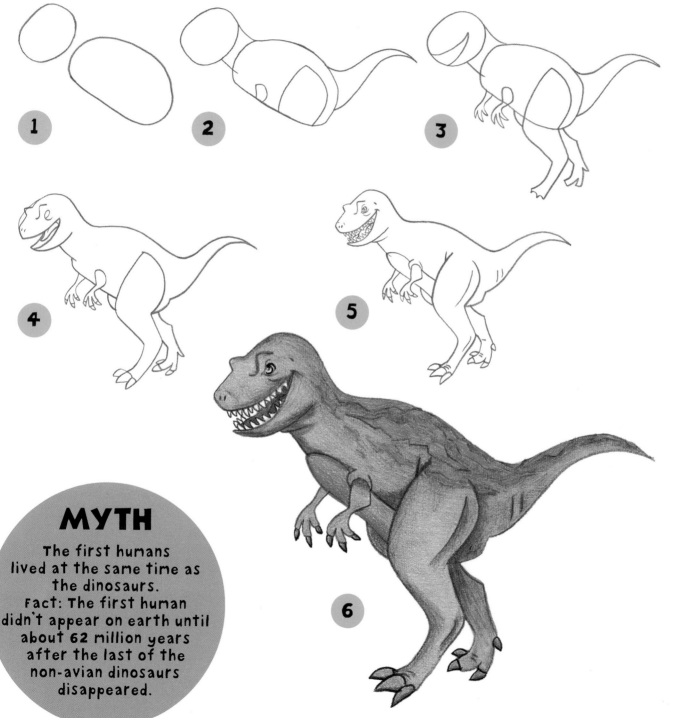

1

2

3

4

5

6

MYTH

The first humans
lived at the same time as
the dinosaurs.
Fact: The first human
didn't appear on earth until
about 62 million years
after the last of the
non-avian dinosaurs
disappeared.

PTERANODON

The Pteranodon was a flying lizard with a tiny sausage-shaped body; a thin, long head with a birdlike beak; and large, batlike wings.

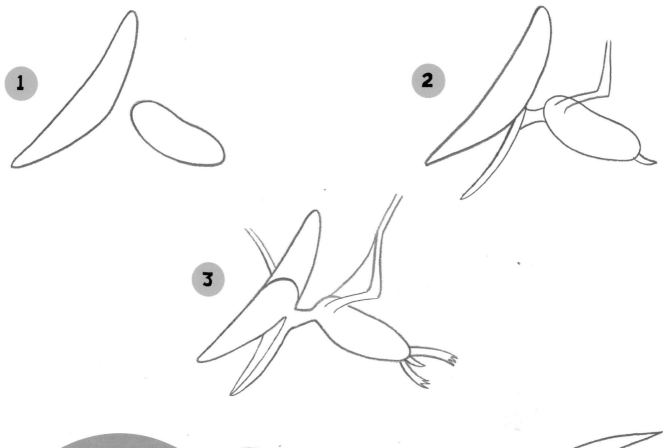

MYTH

An asteroid killed the dinosaurs.
Fact: The latest evidence shows that a large asteroid hit the earth right around the time of the dinosaurs' extinction. But most dinosaur experts believe this is just one of many reasons the dinosaurs died out.

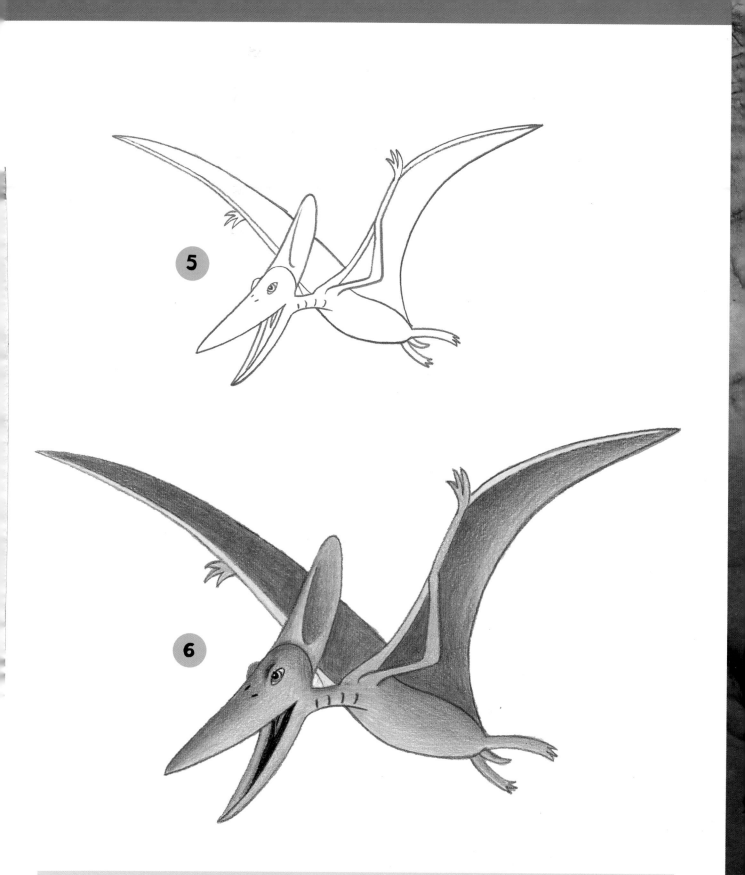

FUN FACT

The Pteranodon belonged to the pterosaurs, a family of flying lizards that lived at the same time as the dinosaurs. The pterosaurs had lightweight bones, but the Pteranodon still weighed 37 pounds. This non-dino needed wings the width of a house (23 feet) to keep it airborne!

PARASAUROLOPHUS

Many dinos had heavy, thick bodies like the Parasaurolophus. But this biped's curved-head crest and duck-billed beak made it unique!

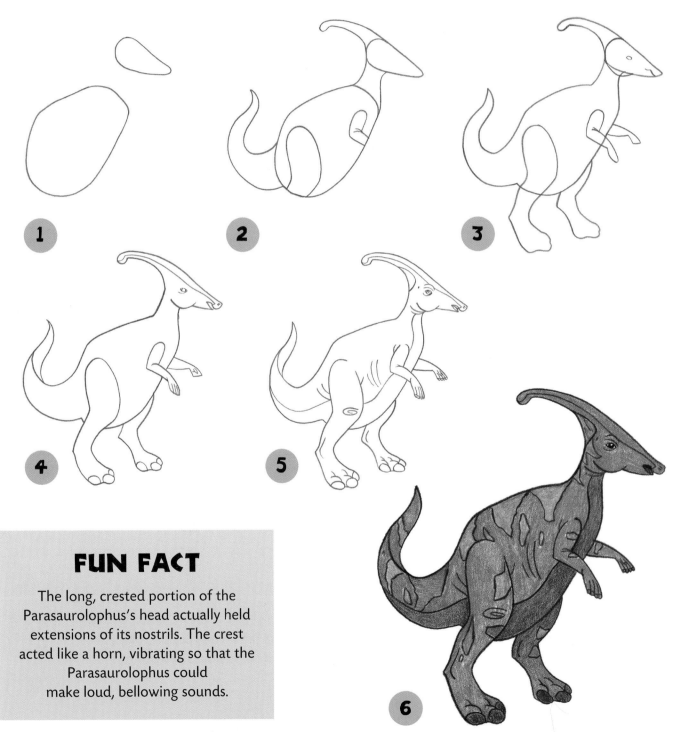

FUN FACT

The long, crested portion of the Parasaurolophus's head actually held extensions of its nostrils. The crest acted like a horn, vibrating so that the Parasaurolophus could make loud, bellowing sounds.

DIPLODOCUS

Draw this enormous sauropod with a large,
oval body and a whiplike tail, but make its head small—
it had a brain the size of a human fist!

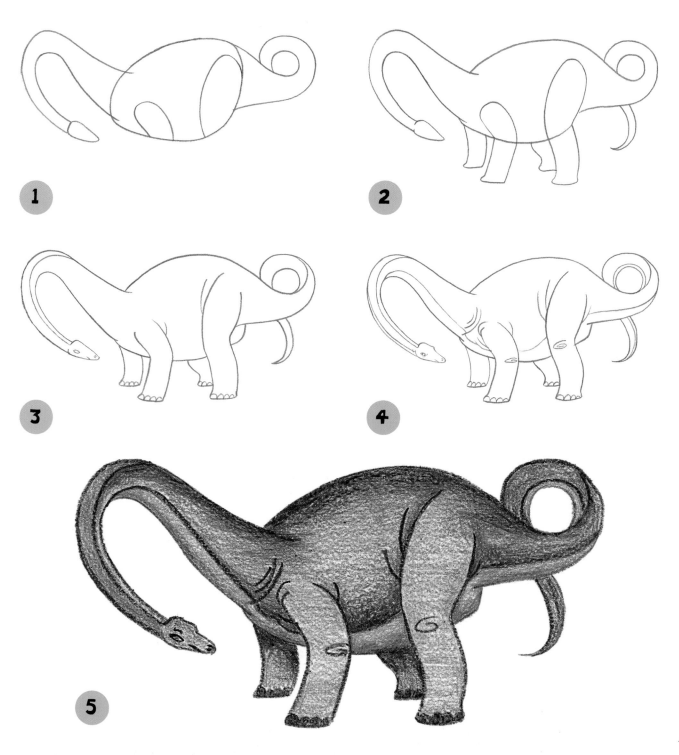

DINO EXTREMES

The prehistoric creatures on these pages are beyond super—they're supreme! As you learn to draw these amazing animals, keep in mind their record-breaking features.

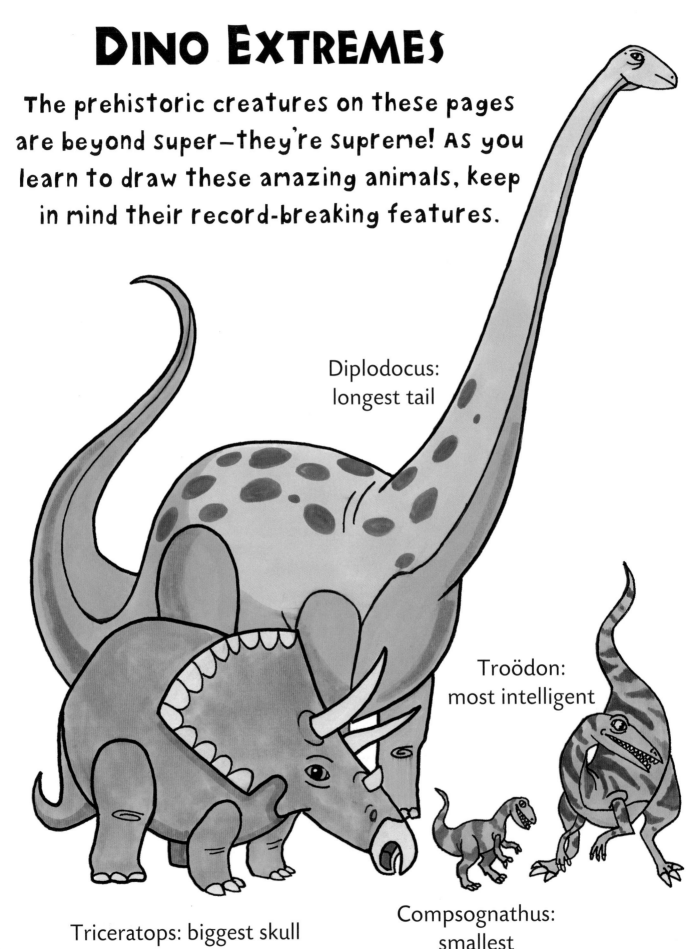

Diplodocus: longest tail

Troödon: most intelligent

Triceratops: biggest skull

Compsognathus: smallest

Quetzalcoatlus:
largest pterosaur

Sauroposeidon:
tallest

Ornithomimus:
fastest

Ankylosaurus:
widest

Maiasaura:
most teeth

STEGOSAURUS

If you can draw your attention away from the row of plates on this stegosaur's back, you might notice its other features—including long, straight hind legs and a powerful, spiked tail.

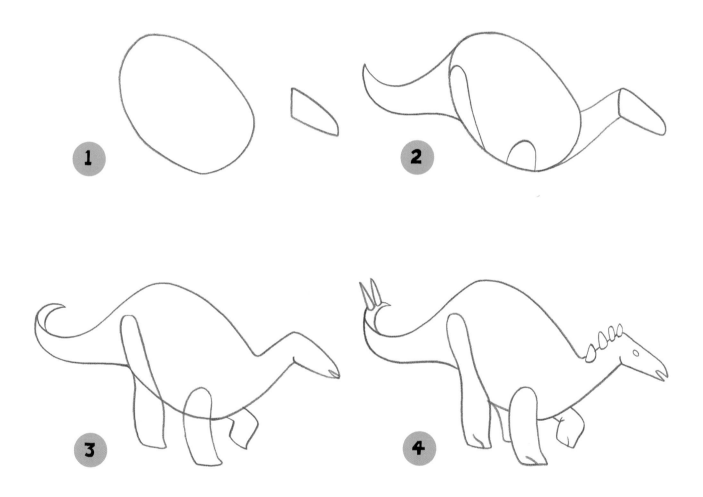

FUN FACT

The Stegosaurus is the largest of the stegosaurs (that is, dinos with bony plates, long hind legs, and small heads). Paleontologists—scientists who study life from prehistoric times—believe that a Stegosaurus would display its plates both to scare off predators and to attract mates.

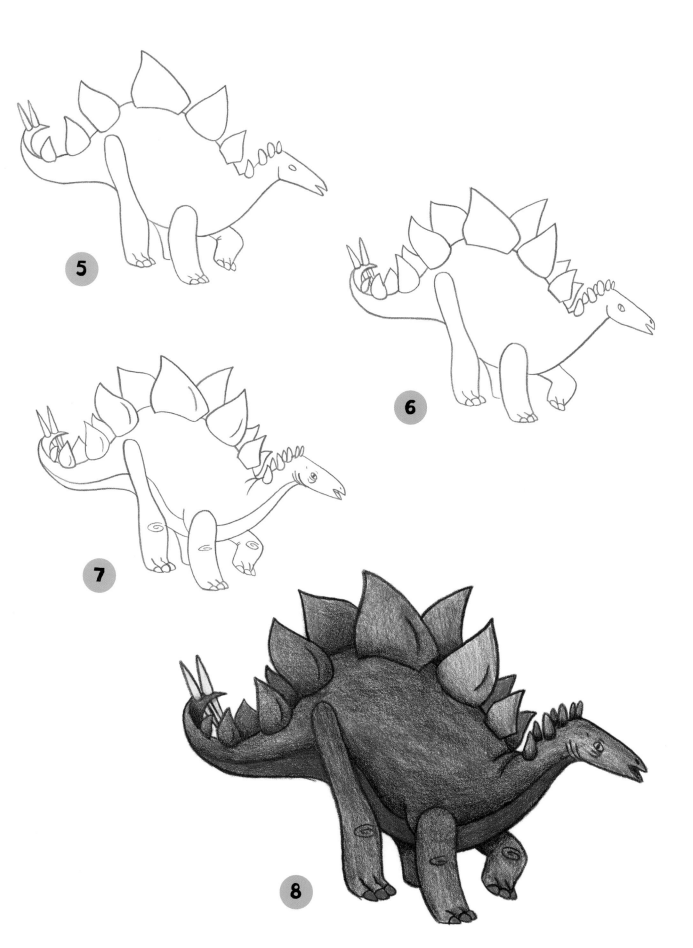

5

6

7

8

MAMENCHISAURUS

The Mamenchisaurus had the longest neck of all the dinos! Its tail and body were also long, but its legs were relatively short.

24

BARYONYX

The highly intelligent Baryonyx used both its large rear legs and smaller "arms" to carry its 2-ton body. Its "smile" resembled a crocodile's.

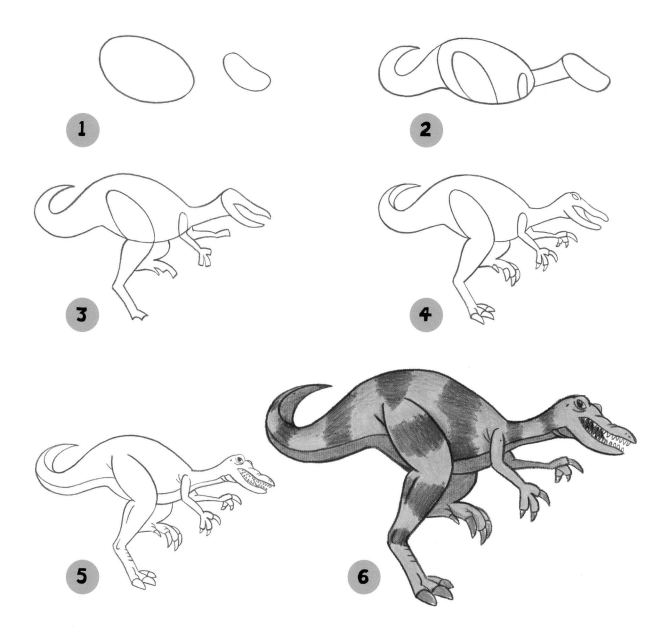

FUN FACT

This biped was named Baryonyx, meaning "heavy claw," for the giant 1-foot-long claws on its "hands." But that wasn't the only dangerous feature of this predator. The Baryonyx also had a jaw lined with 96 super-sharp teeth!

ANKYLOSAURUS

To draw this heavily armored dinosaur, begin with an egg shape for the body and a rounded rectangle for the head. Later add details, including spikes on the club tail and triangle horns on the head!

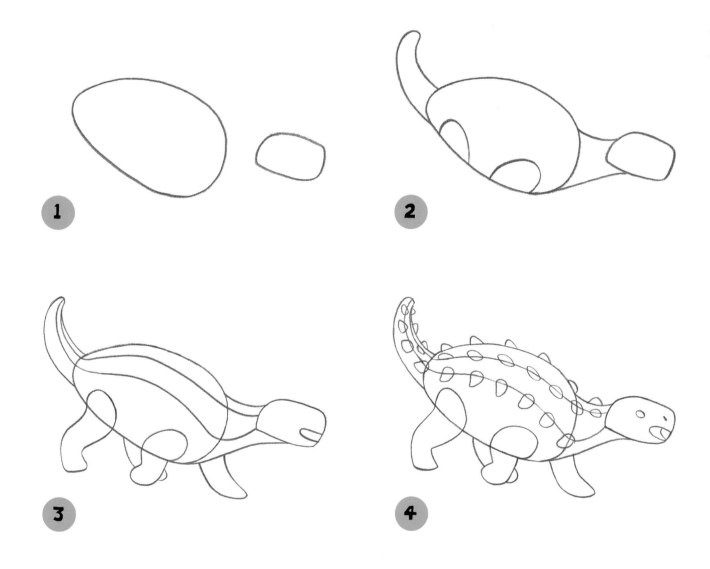

FUN FACT

The Ankylosaurus was thick-headed—in every sense! Its body was heavily layered with armor, making it a well-protected herbivore (or plant eater). But its armored skull was so thick and broad that there was very little room left for a brain!

5

6

7

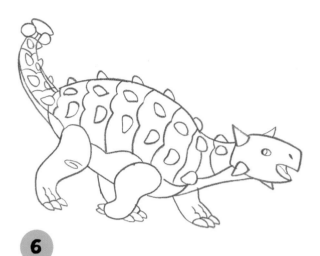

8

VELOCIRAPTOR

Velociraptor means "speedy predator," so it makes sense that this dino had a slim body, sharp claws, and powerful jaws.

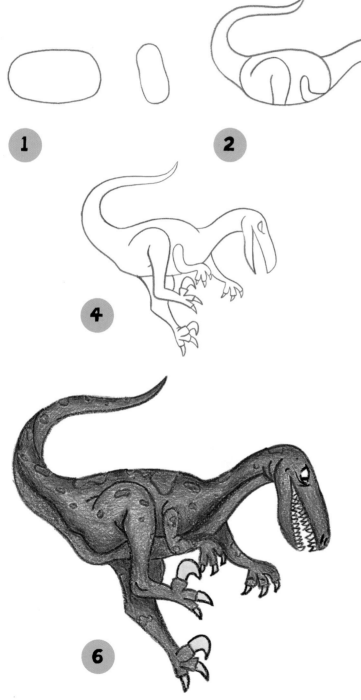

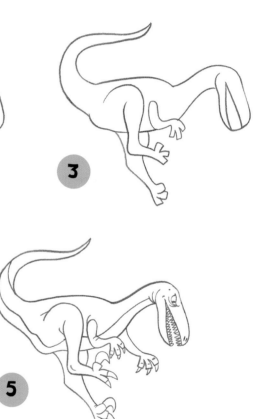

FUN FACT

Paleontologists have discovered much about the Velociraptor's eating and hunting habits because of a rare fossil find. An almost complete Velociraptor skeleton was found preserved in an attack position, still clutching the skull of its prey: a Protoceratops!

MAIASAURA

The Maiasaura walked on all fours, but this herbivore could run quickly using its strong back legs alone. Its thick tail provided balance.

1

2

3

4

5

6

KENTROSAURUS

The small head of the Kentrosaurus was toothless, so its beak was long and thin. This herbivore had sharp spikes on its tail and—like other stegosaurs—bony, triangular plates on its back.

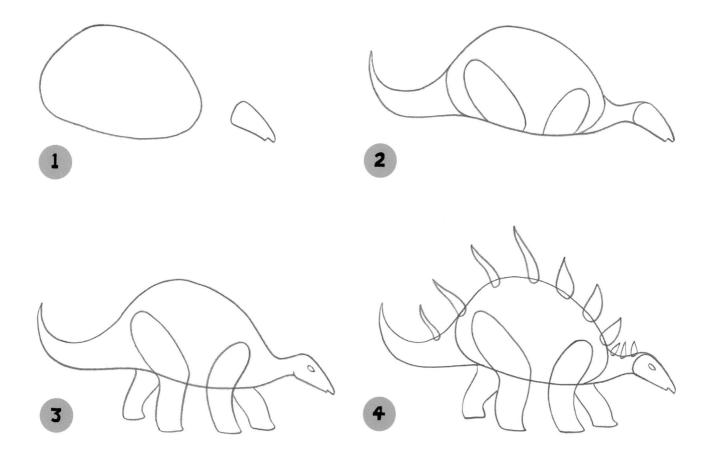

FUN FACT

Although the stegosaurus had one of the lowest levels of intelligence, the Kentrosaurus had a small head that held a brain the size of a walnut. However, the Kentrosaurus brain did have well-developed olfactory bulbs (or scent receptors), which gave the bulky dinosaur an excellent sense of smell.

5

6

7

MYTH

Every dinosaur was either an herbivore or a carnivore. Fact: Although the majority of dinosaurs were exclusively herbivores or carnivores, there were some omnivore dinosaurs. Omnivores are animals that eat both meat and plants.

8

DIMETRODON

This spiny, sail-backed carnivore was
a pelycosaur, a prehistoric animal that roamed
the earth long before the dinosaurs.

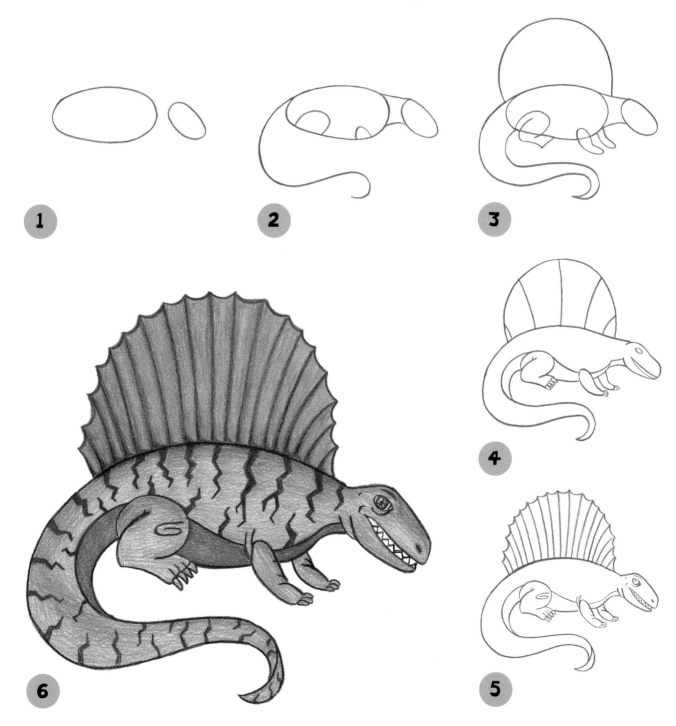

UTAHRAPTOR

When referring to dinosaurs, raptor means "robber." This thief was a predator with powerful, clawed feet and long, grasping "hands."

FUN FACT

In 1991, paleontologists in Utah uncovered the ultra-large Utahraptor. This striking dinosaur was 16 to 23 feet long and weighed up to 1 ton!

SAUROPOSEIDON

can you believe that a 60-foot-tall, 60-ton giraffe-like creature once roamed the earth? Everything about this sauropod was big—from its snaking, 40-foot-long neck to its thick, tree-trunk legs!

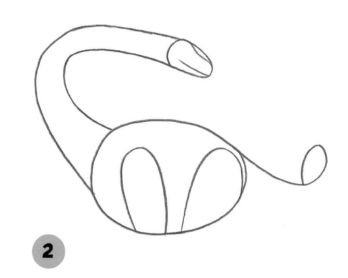

5

FUN FACT

This amazingly large herbivore was named after the Greek god Poseidon, who ruled earthquakes. According to paleontologists, the Sauroposeidon, or "thunder lizard," was so big that even if it had walked very carefully, it would have caused small earthquakes!

6

TRICERATOPS

The bulky Triceratops is best known for its three horns. Draw one long horn above each eye and a third, shorter horn above the snout.

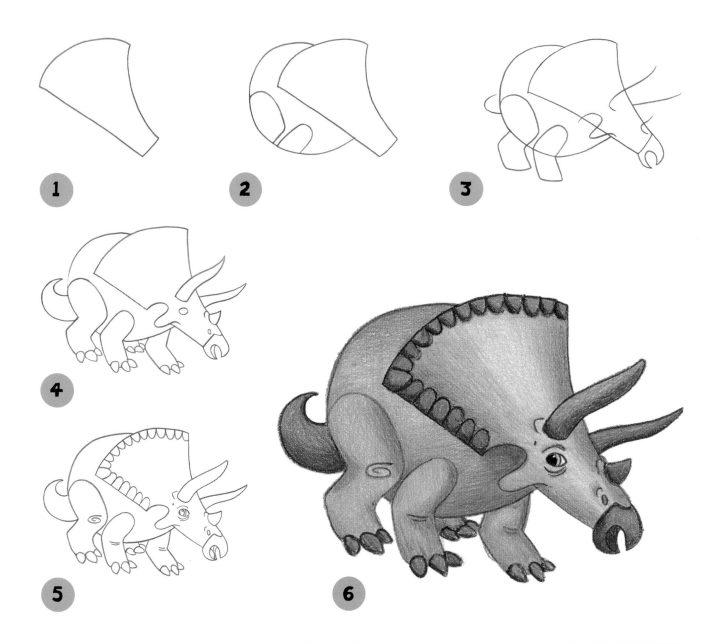

1

2

3

4

5

6

FUN FACT

Its three large horns gave the Triceratops a frightening appearance. But this herbivore probably would have used its horns only in self-defense—or to push over tall trees so it could reach taller branches with tender, delicate leaves.

PACHYCEPHALOSAURUS

The defining feature of this herbivore was its unusual head. Nine inches of bone protected the Pachycephalosaurus's brain. And the special bumps and nodes on its snout helped it root up food.

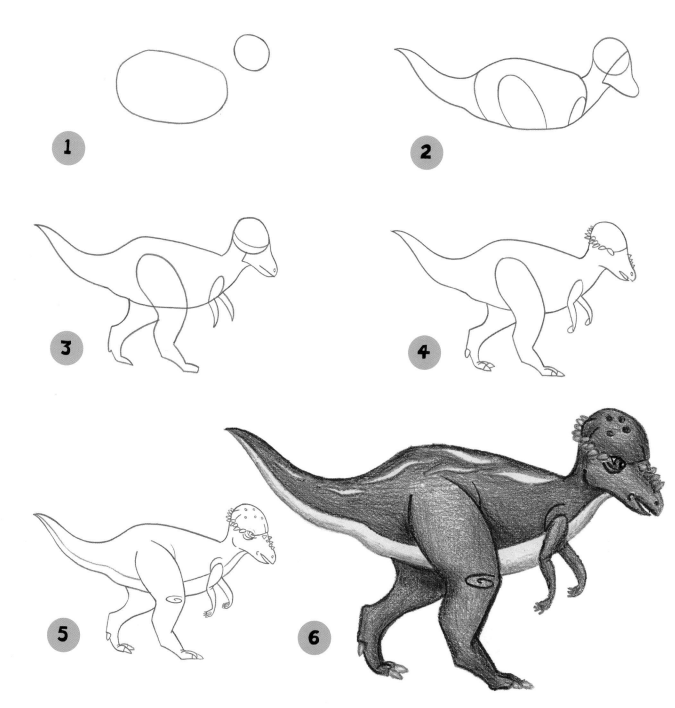

1

2

3

4

5

6

TYRANNOSAURUS

The largest in the family of bipedal carnivores known as theropods, the T-Rex had a big head, powerful legs, and a thick tail.

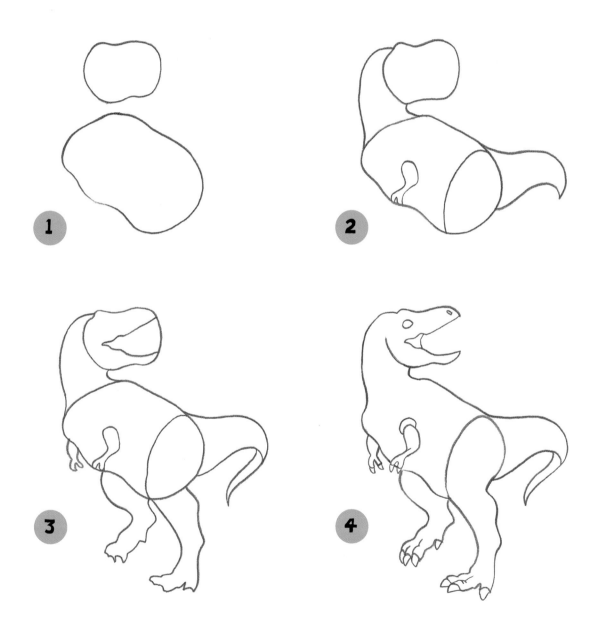

5

6

7

POLACANTHUS

Polacanthus means "many-spined," and there's no better way to describe this four-legged, armor-covered dinosaur!

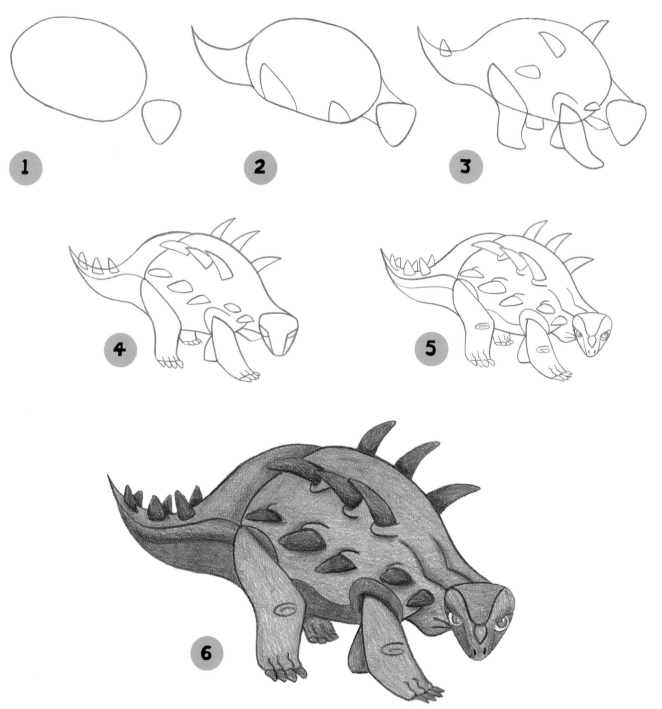